Measuring Time

Months of the Year

Tracey Steffora

Raintree

www.raintreepublishers.co.uk
Visit our website to find out more information about Raintree books.

To order:
Phone 0845 6044371
Fax +44 (0) 1865 312263
Email myorders@raintreepublishers.co.uk

Customers from outside the UK please telephone +44 1865 312262

Raintree is an imprint of Capstone Global Library Limited, a company incorporated in England and Wales having its registered office at 7 Pilgrim Street, London, EC4V 6LB – Registered company number: 6695582

First published in hardback in 2011

Edited by Tracey Steffora, Dan Nunn, and Sian Smith
Designed by Richard Parker
Picture research by Hannah Taylor
Originated by Capstone Global Library Ltd
Printed and bound in China by Leo Paper Products Ltd

ISBN 978 1 406 22305 7
15 14 13 12 11
10 9 8 7 6 5 4 3 2 1

British Library Cataloguing in Publication Data
Steffora, Tracey.
Months of the year. -- (Measuring time)
1. Months--Juvenile literature. 2. Time--Juvenile literature.
I. Title II. Series
529.2-dc22

Acknowledgements
We would like to thank the following for permission to reproduce photographs: Alamy Images pp. **13** (©Greatstock Photographic Library), **16** (©nobleIMAGES), **21** (©Florian Franke); Corbis p. **12** (Radius Images/Jerzyworks); istockphoto pp. **4** (©diego cervo), **5** (©johnnyscriv), **10** (©Simon Greig), **14** (©Gord Horne), **15** (©Dmitry Maslov), **17** (©Sergey Borisov), **23 top** (©Simon Greig); Photolibrary pp. **9** (Blend Images); Rex Features p. **8** (View China Photo); shutterstock pp. **11** (©Karel Gallas), **18** (©Johnny_Walker), **19** (©Lijuan Guo), **20** (©rietephotos) **23 mid** (©Johnny_Walker), **23 bot** (©Lijuan Guo).

Front cover photograph of corkboard with pinned index cards reproduced with permission of istockphoto (©Matt Jeacock). Back cover photograph of young animals reproduced with permission of shutterstock (© Karel Gallas).

Every effort has been made to contact copyright holders of any material reproduced in this book. Any omissions will be rectified in subsequent printings if notice is given to the publisher.

Contents

What is time?

Time is how long something takes.
Time is when things happen.

We measure time in many ways. One way to measure time is in months.

Twelve months

March						
Sunday	Monday	Tuesday	Wednesday	Thursday	Friday	Saturday
		1	2	3	4	5
6	7	8	9	10	11	12
13	14	15	16	17	18	19
20	21	22	23	24	25	26
27	28	29	30	31		

A month is a long time.

Most months are 30 or 31 days.

JANUARY

Sunday	Monday	Tuesday	Wednesday	Thursday	Friday	Saturday
						1
2	3	4	5	6	7	8
9	10	11	12	13	14	15
16	17	18	19	20	21	22
23	24	25	26	27	28	29
30	31					

FEBRUARY

Sunday	Monday	Tuesday	Wednesday	Thursday	Friday	Saturday
		1	2	3	4	5
6	7	8	9	10	11	12
13	14	15	16	17	18	19
20	21	22	23	24	25	26
27	28					

MARCH

Sunday	Monday	Tuesday	Wednesday	Thursday	Friday	Saturday
		1	2	3	4	5
6	7	8	9	10	11	12
13	14	15	16	17	18	19
20	21	22	23	24	25	26
27	28	29	30	31		

APRIL

Sunday	Monday	Tuesday	Wednesday	Thursday	Friday	Saturday
					1	2
3	4	5	6	7	8	9
10	11	12	13	14	15	16
17	18	19	20	21	22	23
24	25	26	27	28	29	30

MAY

Sunday	Monday	Tuesday	Wednesday	Thursday	Friday	Saturday
1	2	3	4	5	6	7
8	9	10	11	12	13	14
15	16	17	18	19	20	21
22	23	24	25	26	27	28
29	30	31				

JUNE

Sunday	Monday	Tuesday	Wednesday	Thursday	Friday	Saturday
			1	2	3	4
5	6	7	8	9	10	11
12	13	14	15	16	17	18
19	20	21	22	23	24	25
26	27	28	29	30		

JULY

Sunday	Monday	Tuesday	Wednesday	Thursday	Friday	Saturday
					1	2
3	4	5	6	7	8	9
10	11	12	13	14	15	16
17	18	19	20	21	22	23
24	25	26	27	28	29	30
31						

AUGUST

Sunday	Monday	Tuesday	Wednesday	Thursday	Friday	Saturday
	1	2	3	4	5	6
7	8	9	10	11	12	13
14	15	16	17	18	19	20
21	22	23	24	25	26	27
28	29	30	31			

SEPTEMBER

Sunday	Monday	Tuesday	Wednesday	Thursday	Friday	Saturday
				1	2	3
4	5	6	7	8	9	10
11	12	13	14	15	16	17
18	19	20	21	22	23	24
25	26	27	28	29	30	

OCTOBER

Sunday	Monday	Tuesday	Wednesday	Thursday	Friday	Saturday
						1
2	3	4	5	6	7	8
9	10	11	12	13	14	15
16	17	18	19	20	21	22
23	24	25	26	27	28	29
30	31					

NOVEMBER

Sunday	Monday	Tuesday	Wednesday	Thursday	Friday	Saturday
		1	2	3	4	5
6	7	8	9	10	11	12
13	14	15	16	17	18	19
20	21	22	23	24	25	26
27	28	29	30			

DECEMBER

Sunday	Monday	Tuesday	Wednesday	Thursday	Friday	Saturday
				1	2	3
4	5	6	7	8	9	10
11	12	13	14	15	16	17
18	19	20	21	22	23	24
25	26	27	28	29	30	31

A year is a longer time.

There are 12 months in a year.

January
February
March
April
May
June
July
August
September
October
November
December

January is the first month.
We say "Happy New Year" in January.

January
February
March
April
May
June
July
August
September
October
November
December

February is the shortest month.
It has 28 or 29 days.

January
February
March
April
May
June
July
August
September
October
November
December

March, April, and May are spring months in many places.

The days get warmer.

Baby animals are born in spring.

January
February
March
April
May
June
July
August
September
October
November
December

June, July, and August are summer months in many places.

It is warm in summer. There is more daylight than darkness.

January
February
March
April
May
June
July
August
September
October
November
December

September, October, and November are autumn months in many places.

The days get colder. Some animals gather food for winter.

January
February
March
April
May
June
July
August
September
October
November
December

December is the last month. December is a winter month in many places.

It is cold in winter. There is more darkness than daylight in winter.

Look around you

Each month, the Moon looks different
at different times.

Look at the shape of the Moon on different nights.

Chinese New Year

Special things happen every month.

What special things do you do each month?

Leap year

Month	Number of days
January	31 days
February	28 or 29 days
March	31 days
April	30 days
May	31 days
June	30 days
July	31 days
August	31 days
September	30 days
October	31 days
November	30 days
December	31 days

A leap year happens every four years. February has 29 days in a leap year.

Picture glossary

daylight sunlight, or light during the day

Moon object in space that moves around the Earth

night the time of day when there is no sunlight

Index

Notes for parents and teachers

Before reading

Review the months of the year. Make a timeline of the twelve months and ask the children to record their birthdays on the timeline. Discuss other events that happen over the course of a year and also record them on the timeline.

After reading

Find an example of a moon phase calendar, or a calendar that illustrates the different phases of the Moon. Discuss with the children how we see different parts of the Moon's surface illuminated over the course of a month. If possible, encourage them to look at the Moon every night and report what they observe.